IMPERFECTIONS

SWIKRITI MANDHYAN

Copyright © Swikriti Mandhyan
All Rights Reserved.

ISBN 978-1-68554-316-7

This book has been published with all efforts taken to make the material error-free after the consent of the author. However, the author and the publisher do not assume and hereby disclaim any liability to any party for any loss, damage, or disruption caused by errors or omissions, whether such errors or omissions result from negligence, accident, or any other cause.

While every effort has been made to avoid any mistake or omission, this publication is being sold on the condition and understanding that neither the author nor the publishers or printers would be liable in any manner to any person by reason of any mistake or omission in this publication or for any action taken or omitted to be taken or advice rendered or accepted on the basis of this work. For any defect in printing or binding the publishers will be liable only to replace the defective copy by another copy of this work then available.

Dedicated to my past self, my present and my future

Contents

Prologue   *vii*

1. Chapter 1 — 1
2. Chapter 2 — 2
3. Chapter 3 — 4
4. Chapter 4 — 5
5. Chapter 5 — 7
6. Chapter 6 — 8
7. Chapter 7 — 9
8. Chapter 8 — 10
9. Chapter 9 — 11
10. Chapter 10 — 13
11. Chapter 11 — 14
12. Chapter 12 — 15
13. Chapter 13 — 16
14. Chapter 14 — 18
15. Chapter 15 — 19
16. Chapter 16 — 20
17. Chapter 17 — 21
18. Chapter 18 — 22
19. Chapter 19 — 23
20. Chapter 20 — 24
21. Chapter 21 — 25
22. Chapter 22 — 26
23. Chapter 23 — 27

Contents

24. Chapter 24	28
25. Chapter 25	29
26. Chapter 26	30
27. Chapter 27	31
28. Chapter 28	33
29. Chapter 29	34
30. Chapter 30	35
31. Chapter 31	36
32. Chapter 32	37
33. Chapter 33	39
34. Chapter 34	40
35. Chapter 35	41
36. Chapter 36	42
37. Chapter 37	43
38. Chapter 38	44
39. Chapter 39	47

Prologue

An ode to everyone who feels alone in the presence of their old antagonist, life.

Chapter1

I planted a bunch of flowers
To give to people each day
Everyone I gave a flower to
Had a smile brought to their face
Inside all of the flowers
Were pieces of my soul
No one gives me flowers
So, I give them to make me whole
I wondered if I gave enough flowers would someone give me one
To prove that someone actually cared
About the good that I had done
So, I gave people flowers
The ones that my soul had grown
I failed to notice that the prettiest flowers
Are the one that grow alone
If you could see your soul tonight,
How much would you grieve
For the dage
It has suffered
At the hands of those
Who treated it so cruelly?

Chapter 2

You are not your age,
nor the size of clothes you wear,
You are not a weight,
or the color of your hair.
You are not your name,
or the dimples in your cheeks.
You are all the books you read,
and all the words you speak.
You are your croaky morning voice,
and the smiles you try to hide.
You're the sweetness in your laughter,
and every tear you've cried.
You're the songs you sing so loudly,
when you know you're all alone.
You're the places that you've been to,
and the one that you call home.
You're the things that you believe in,
and the people whom you love.
You're the photos in your bedroom,
and the future you dream of.
You're made of so much beauty,
but it seems that you forgot

SWIKRITI MANDHYAN

*When you decided that you were defined,
by all the things you're not.*

Chapter3

If you go outside at night,
After the world has gone to sleep,
You can hear the Planet sigh,
Under the secrets it can't keep,
And the wind sings different tunes,
To all the ones you hear by day,
As though it's choking on the Words,
That we're all too afraid to say,
And I wonder at the problems,
We've tried to melt inside its core,
Whether it's packed so close to bursting,
That it can't hold many more, for how can we see its weakness,
When we've not known something so strong,
And if it weeps and we can't hear it, does that mean there's
nothing wrong?

Chapter 4

I saw it once,
I have no doubt;
but now can't place
its whereabouts."
"I try to think it,
time and time;
but what it is,
won't come to mind."
"A word, a scent-
a feeling, a past.
It will not show,
though much I've asked."
"And when it comes,
I soon forget-
this is how I felt,
when we first met."
I look back and realise
That i clung on when
I should have let go
And let go
When i should have
Clung on for

IMPERFECTIONS

Dear life

Chapter5

Roses aren't always red
And violets aren't exactly blue,
The society that we live in
never seems to speak the truth.
Smiles aren't always happy
and frowns aren't always upset,
People judge too quickly
and our feelings are what they forget.

Chapter 6

Brown Eyes
Her eyes are blue
Yours are brown
\Hers represents the ocean
Yours represents the ground
You've always hated your eyes
And wished that they were blue
But your eyes have a tint of gold
So rare it must not be true
So yes her eyes are blue
And yes your eyes are brown
But your eyes hold the riches
That are buried in the ground
Her eyes carry storms
And rage like the sea
Your eyes carry earthquakes
That bring mountains to their knees
Maybe her eyes are blue
But your eyes reign queen
Because they hold the purest riches
The world has ever seen

Chapter 7

I add sorry to the end of my sentences
As if I'm sorry for what I say
My words are a form of protection
That I must strip away
I must always be quiet
And I can't make any demands
When I speak, I must be careful
That all my words are planned
For my words are a weapon
One that I can never use
And when everything is gone
They are the last thing I can lose
To protect my very being
I must never speak too loud
If I ever do speak
I will barely make a sound
So I always say sorry
As if my words burn me
My words are my own prison
And I can never be free

Chapter 8

Welcome to society,
We hope you enjoy your stay,
And please feel free to be yourself,
As long as it's in the right way,
Make sure you love your body,
Not too much or we'll tear you down,
We'll bully you for smiling,
And then wonder why you frown,
We'll tell you that you're worthless,
That you shouldn't make a sound,
And then cry with all the others,
As you're buried in the ground,
You can fall in love with anyone,
As long as it's who we choose
And we'll let you have your opinions,
But please shape them to our views,
Welcome to society,
We promise that we won't deceive,
And one more rule now that you're here,
There's no way you can leave.

Chapter 9

They say happiness will find you,
But I think sadness will find you too,
It sneaks up on you in darkness,
Just when you think you've made it through,
It opens holes in what was solid ground,
The kind you never know are there,
Until you go to take another step,
And find you're standing over the air,
The world around you passes by,
In blurs of color and sound,
Nothing around you making sense,
As you continue you plummet down,
You can't remember how it started,
And you don't know when it will end,
But you know that you'd give anything,
To stand up on your feet again,
Sadness is that feeling,
When the falling doesn't stop,
And it saps your life of meaning,
And of the good things that you've got,
So when you finally hit rock bottom,
And you look back at the sky,

IMPERFECTIONS

What you once has seems so far away,
The only thing left t do is cry,
People all yell out "save yourself
Calling things about "happiness" and "hope"
But they 're too busy with their lives to realize,
It 'd be a lot quicker if they let down a rope.

Chapter10

I am broken and I can't be fixed,
I miss you but will I be missed?
I am fighting a battle
That I will never win.
It's all wounded and broken,
I can't let you in so don't come close,
I am torn apart by you and
I can't take it anymore,
My soul fell in love with you
And you led me to the way to some other world.

Chapter 11

Our mothers tell us that
There are no monsters
Under our beds,
Or hidden inside our closets
But they don't warn us
that sometimes monsters
Come dressed as people that claim to love you more than sun
loves the moon

Chapter12

So many people walk the earth,
With purpose in their eyes,
But in their heart of hearts they know,
What they're living is a lie,
The alarm goes off 6AM,
Like every other day,
So they can walk into a job they hate,
Because they need pay,
All time does is take from them,
But it never seems to give,
Always waiting for the day to come,
When they finally start to live,
I'm all too scared that one day son,
I'll become just like the rest,
Only walking with the crowd,
Because my dreams have been oppressed,
That one day I'll look back on life,
At the opportunities that I missed,
And realize I never truly lived,
All I did was just exist.

Chapter 13

After a while
you learn
the subtle difference between
holding a hand and chaining a soul
and you learn love doesn't mean leaning
and company doesn't always mean security.
And you begin to learn
that kisses aren't contracts and
presents aren't always promises
and you begin to accept your defeats
with your head up and your eyes ahead
with the grace of a woman,
not the grief of a child.
And you learn
to build all your roads on today
because tomorrow's ground is
too uncertain for plans and futures have
a way of falling down in mid-flight.
After a while you learn
that even sunshine burns
if you get too much
So you plant your own garden

SWIKRITI MANDHYAN

and decorate your own soul
instead of waiting
for someone to bring you flowers

Chapter 14

The moon taught me
There is beauty
In darkness too,
That even when
I don't feel whole,
I am enough

Chapter 15

We enter the woods
As a children
Lured by adventure
We lingered
As teens
Lost in the underbrush
We see the forest
As adults
Rooted in our ways

Chapter 16

He is a storm,
and storms devastate,
but every time he hurts you,
you hold your breath
and bear the hurricane;
repeating to yourself
One more chance
One more breath
just one more,
and you'll fix him
Until one day you can't
hold your breath anymore,
and you are half a stormy evening,
one tearstained night,
two minutes
and five seconds
away from breaking down.
And you realise,
you fix anyone,
not until you fix yourself.

Chapter 17

She,
In the dark,
Found light,
Brighter than many ever see,
She,
Within herself,
Found loveliness,
Through the soul's own mastery,
And now the world receives
From her dower:
The message of the strength
Of inner power

Chapter18

Who knows,
That I the depth of the ravine
Of the mountain of my hidden heart
A firefly of my love is aflame.

Chapter19

Do you know what you are?
You are a manuscript
Of a divine letter
You are a mirror
Reflecting a noble face.
This universe is
Not outside of you.
Look inside yourself;
Everything that you want,
you are already that.

Chapter 20

I miss the excitement I miss having arms around me
As our laughs twirl around the air
I miss the way a touch can speak when words aren't
Enough,
How hands become artists,
Painting my body,
From head to toe,
Caressing my face,
Tracing my spine;
It made me feel alive;
But now
I'm scared of being touched,
and not because of their touch hurt,
But because of how much it hurts
When their touch stops.

Chapter 21

She speaks to me fondly of passions and talents,
guitars and stars, and then stops short
and apologizes for speaking at all.
All because somewhere in her life,
someone she loved broke her heart
by ignoring her beautiful words and
telling her to shut up,
keep it down, nobody cares.
People aren't born sad.
We make them that way.

Chapter22

The moon is drink
And the stars intoxicated,
With the sins of the sun,
And the sadness of the sky,
Shifts, blurs from the earth,
And you stare,
And wonder why the universe,
Never loved you back.

Chapter 23

We are not haunted by the dead.
We are haunted by the living
and the graveyard of memories
they leave in our heads.

Chapter 24

I am the girl
No one looked
Twice at,
I'm not popular,
I'm known,
I don't
Have a million
Friends,
I have 2
I'm pretty
But not
Gorgeous,
I am likable
Not
Loveable,
And I'm in the background
Character,
Not the main one.
And u was a fool
to think you
thought any
Different.

Chapter 25

WHAT THE NIGHT SAYS
The darkness says: it's night.
The stars say: shine.
Fantasy says: its magic
The valley says: no, it's mine.
Mystery says: it's all a puzzle
The dream gatherer says: I'm fading
The moonlight: I'm dissolved
Memory days: remember.
Demonica shouts out: scream!
The awakening whispers: sunrise.
The night says: it's all a dream

Chapter 26

It's not the endings that will haunt you
But the space where they should lie,
The things that simply faded
Without one final wave goodbye.
Like a book with torn out pages,
Forgetting things you're sure you knew,
A question with no answers
And a song stopped halfway through.
So when your mind attempts to store them
Their crooked shape will never fit,
And forever in the corners
Of your consciousness they sit.
Jagged edges made from moments
You can't be quite sure were the last,
Slicing open thoughts that healed
As they attempt to slip right past.
You see, not knowing is what haunts you,
The memories that never mend,
For they are puzzles missing pieces
Of all the things that didn't.

Chapter27

You said you couldn't keep waiting,
for me to say "I love you".
But I'd said it to you every day,
in ways you never even knew,
It blown over the song that,
I sang for you in boring time,
Caught in the way I kissed your bruises,
just to take away the pain,
Baked in the French Fries I bought you
when you got the last piece.
And in the ways that I would miss you
every time that you were gone.
Sipped in every breath I took
when you laid down your head on my shoulder
and my arms surrounded your waist.
I might not have said those three words
in the old and standard way.
But I'd learnt actions speak much louder
than anything that you can say.
So if you're really tired of waiting
for those three words to leave my throat,
all I can say is that it's cold outside,

IMPERFECTIONS

so don't forget your coat.

Chapter 28

Float towards the moon
Settling on the surface
Observing the earth below
Fire fills the green
Pollutants fill the blue
I, too, am filled with fire and pollutants
Closer to earth than
I've imagined
poisoning my home
Without caution of the damage
So, as I look closer
I see a field of flowers
Ready to bloom
Just as I am,
Jumping from the moon
Into the ocean blue
Blooming a new part of me
Using the refreshing waves
To wash over the past
And nourish me
For a new beginning.

Chapter 29

What colour are her eyes?
They are the colour
Of tawny whiskey; intense,
Spicy cinnamon hue
Speckled with gold
Tuscan earth tones
Of sienna and umber
And when the light
Shines on them
Copper pools of fire.

Chapter 30

You loved me like a flower
The ones you leave to die
Instead of loving me wild
You kept me locked inside
You let me slowly wilt
Until there was only a piece of who I was
And keeping something wild, locked
You should see what it does
If you meet a girl like me
I ask you to let her go
So you can see what happens
When you let a flower grow
And I did not get that choice
But I do not blame it all on you
And I let you take me away
Because I thought you were beautiful too
It is true you broke me
But I still wish you well
And I hope I was beautiful
Before my petals fell

Chapter31

Because no matter the amount of times
you have felt lost
In a sea of a thousand things to do,
A range of roles and responsibilities
And the many ways that others see you,
All along, you have still been you
Yoh have been blooming everyday.
And no amount of feeling unnoticed
Can pull you away
From this truth

Chapter 32

She smelled of books and stories,
Of all the worlds she'd lived within,
As though the ink had left the pages,
To find a new home in her skin,
She didn't quite belong here,
Lived a life within her head,
Like she'd slipped out from the covers,
Of a paperback instead,
And you'd see it in her eyes
That they were deeper than a well,
She was a whole library of stories,
That we'd beg for her to tell,
When she spoke the world would listen,
To the adventures of her mind,
For if there's such thing as magic,
Then it was something she could find,
And her heart had looked much further,
Then her eyes had ever seen,
She'd walked on words to places,
Her two feet had never been,
It's years now since she moved,
And we all failed to keep in touch,

IMPERFECTIONS

So, her memory's all faded,
Like a book you've read too much,
But if she hoped to leave us ink-stained,
She should know she did succeed
For even now we all still look for her,
In every book we read.

Chapter 33

The world is a scary place,
And it isn't always nice,
But my child you have a gift,
So let me give you some advice,
You hold the world in your hands,
I know it can seem like a lot,
But my god you move mountains,
And you do it without a thought,
The stars bow down before you,
The sea rises and falls as you breathe,
If you tried you could bring kingdoms,
Crashing to their knees,
But my child you have this light,
I can see it in your eyes,
Don't ever doubt your power,
I know that you will rise
This is my advice,
You are pure and true,
Show the world what you're made of,
Because it doesn't deserve you.

Chapter34

You have shed
A thousand skins
To become the person you are today
And if you ever feel
Overwhelmed
By the many people
You once were,
Remember,
Your bones have grown,
But what makes them
Has never changed

Chapter35

Who told you that your shyness
doesn't make you strong?
who told you that the way you are
is limited and wrong?
Inside you lies a silent strength
That rests behind your eyes.
It can notice people bluffing and
can see between two lies.
Your quirt is a shield with which
you guard a loyal heart
And in a world full of false-heartedness
The way you guard it is an art
Shyness doesn't mean that you
don't live your life out loud;
It means that you have strength
And for that i hope you're proud

Chapter36

I submitted my soul and body
To you to dissolve in your love
Forgotten the throngs
Drenched in the dreams of our sphere
Satisfying our desires
And expressing our love in every possible way
We are getting older together

Fantasies,adoration, affection
Are OUR things
And when i come back to reality
I can't wait to meet you
You have got me
Was waiting for a lifetime for you

I don't know why you are always stuck on my mind
And i am tongue tied over three words,
cursed

Chapter 37

I was looking at the sky today when I realised something. Life is nothing but moments. That fight you had with your friend is just a moment. The night you were up all night finishing a project is just a moment. The night you watched the sunset alone was just a moment. The football championship that you lost in school is just a moment. Every up and every down and everything in between is just a moment that passes with time. You may remember these moments and you may not but what you will remember is the people you spent time with and the way you felt. The way he made you laugh and the way they made you feel like you were on top of the world when you were no where but with your friends and family. All of these moments and feelings and people combine to make up a bigger moment that we call life. Our life is just a moment appreciate the moment you've been given and the people you've been given to spend it with, because no matter how beautiful or tragic a moment is it always ends. So hold on a little tighter, smile a little bigger , cry a little harder, laugh a little louder, forgive a little quicker, and love a whole lot deeper because these are the moments you'll remember when you're old and wishing you could rewind time. Not a single thing lasts forever and thats life.

Chapter 38

Its 5:37 in the morning. Can't sleep. Another restless night. Not a bright start to my day.

Its been 37 days since the last time I heard her voice. 49 days since I saw her face, held her hand and kissed her cheeks. According to her calculations, I should've been doing well by now. Calculations can be wrong, specially when done by a girl. She's doing pretty well I guess. Why not me? Why am I writing this? Questions I have no answer to.

My first break-up. Its not that I was dying to achieve it and am very proud of it, I just didn't realise it would happen to me. I guess nobody does, so lost in each other's love. One doesn't really give it ample thought as long as the fake promises and lies keeps the other at bay. Atleast it was true for me.

To wake up every f*king morning and think of her is a torment. Every morning I wake up and my first thoughts are, 'S*t! Another day! How am I gonna pass this? I should stop thinking about her. She doesn't care for me. I shouldn't too. I must be strong. I miss her. Miss her voice, her hands in mine, her suppressed smile, that funny mark on her face, that nodding of her head to every agreement, that face she makes to every dislike, her tiny cute nose and some traces of hair on it, the dark lines under her eyes…her kiss…everything.'

Suddenly I feel my fingers curling on their own and trying to grip hers. I realise she's not here. Never will be again. At that instant, it feels all the oxygen has been sucked from my room. I struggle to breathe,literally. Sometimes, my eyes get watery. It makes me weaker, physically and mentally, everyday of my life. Then I tell myself ,'Don't worry, just get up now. Don't think of her. You are a very good man. You deserve better. Everything will be alright.' I hope so.

The same story repeats the next morning. Every morning. I wish I could foresee what was coming for me. No. I would not stop loving her then. I would just be more prepared for all this. She was prepared and took me off-guard. If I knew I would make each day with her count.

I can't explain the s**t going through my head. I try to understand where did everything go wrong. Look for that one big reason which made her do it. I can't stop thinking about it. Can't let it go too.

What have I become? A psycho? Clearly I have become obsessed with her. Is it love? What is love to her? Is it care? Will she ever realise how much I love her? I can't think of all these together. It kills me. It is killing me.

I didn't know break-up would be so easy for her and so disastrous for me. I still can't believe it. It has clearly broken me beyond repair. For her it was simply like wishing good morning over the phone. For me it has been my worst nightmare. I wish I could delete just that one day from my life, just that one day.

She once said 'Love is something which 2 people feel good for sometime... feel right'.

'Sometime' was too short in my case. Did she ever love me? Have I been used? Or am I intolerable and a pathetic person?

Unlike her I considered her more than a girlfriend. Loving someone too much can be one's undoing. This should be the first lesson in school. I can only regret now.

She doesn't even want to hear my voice or see me. What does she think of me now? I don't know that. Rather, I don't want to know that. My heart can only take so much. But I'm still holding on to her memories. They are all I have of her. Sweet as well as bitter memories.

I don't know what happens to me next. My life is hanging on uncertainity. Will things turn out fine or will I be an unlucky soul?

Sometimes, only sometimes, I imagine her smiling face and it makes me smile. I remember anything funny she said and it makes my heart lighter. But all this lasts only for a few seconds, because soon after I am overcome with unbearable pain. I just lie on my bed till the pain subsides and try to put on a fake smile.

But, unfortunately, I'm not so good at faking happy tears.

Chapter 39

You came home today, after ditching our date. It wasn't the first time. I was waiting for you neatly dressed for a half day. But there was no sign of you coming into the house. I anticipated your visit so much that I even hallucinated the keys jingle and the door creak open. After a boatload of hallucinations, here you are.

"She needed me. Her boyfriend broke up with her" you said scratching your neck, trying to get the guilt in your eyes. But who are you kidding? I would know your true emotions right away. You didn't feel any guilt or regret, you were just trying not to hurt me.

"I can't do this anymore " I said the things I have been vanquishing myself with. The things which have been making me jittery.

"You always ran to her when she needed you, but what about me? Don't I need you?"

I asked and your brown orbs just twitched. Oh, how bad I desire that they were sad. But nothing. They were just vacuous.

"I can't stay with you anymore, Jake "I said and left your place. I took my luggage and went

to a place that could provide me solace, the park. But I regret going there. There you were, on your best friend's lap. Both of you

giggling to each other. I saw it coming, but why does it hurt this much?
Your friends were mine too. I was invited to some party. I decided to come just so I could get a small glimpse of you. And I did. But again, I regretted it.
There she was. Your best friend, in your arms. You were introducing her to all our friends as your girlfriend. Has it even been two weeks? You could move on that easily. Or maybe you never loved me.

"Jake ,I feel so insecure with your friend. She always looks at you like she is gonna snatch you away from me"
"You're just being paranoid. You know that I'm yours" and then the giggles and the kisses.
Oh, sure I was just paranoid. And no, she didn't snatch you away from me, you willingly let her do that. You didn't care about all my pleas of insecurities. You just let her have you. At this point, I can't help but think that you let her do whatever she wanted to, including nab you away from me.
"I promise you that you are the only girl who owns and rules my heart. She is just someone important to me, but not as important as you" you said while I was crying my heart out.
Maybe I did the right thing by breaking off things. Because you weren't the one to cherish me. You could never do that. You convinced me. For a minute I thought that you were sincere. But all that came crashing down when I saw the apologetic look on your face while you were talking on call to her.

It was all fake. You feigned your assurances.
But I still had a small hope that you would put me above her.
Maybe someday, I would be as important as her to you.

"I love you more than I ever loved anyone Sage " But, was it true at all, Jake ? Did you love me more than her? Because it as sure as hell don't look like it.
"I love you more Jake" I meant it. Even if you didn't, I meant it. I cherished every moment I spent with you because they were quite rare. I loved you more than anything.
I still love you so much that I hope someday you will magically be knocking on my door and then take me into your arms and tell this is all a dream.
But, is that even possible now?

I heard my doorbell ring, indicating I had got a mail. I opened the mail and saw that it was a small wedding card. I should've refrained myself from opening the invitation when I had that unsettling feeling in my gut, but I didn't. I had that curiosity to open it.
It was not just any wedding invitation. It was yours. With your supposed love, your best friend. I felt my heart getting squeezed out but tears refused to come out of my eyes.
I slowly felt my hands losing their grip on the paper. I could feel that immense pain in my heart, which was not alleviated even after drinking a whole glass of water. I decided to give myself some rest and sleep. I laid down but I couldn't sleep. Then, I felt

the tears in my eyes, fall down, drop by drop, sinking into the pillow.

"This seems so hard, is it ever gonna get better?" said one side of my mind.

"Everything will get better eventually; this too shall pass" said the other side of my mind.

I had to be the one to comfort myself because no one knows me better than I do.

A reflection of myself , through scars , flaws and imperfections to self love and admiration. Through loud silent cries and nights to brighter cheerful days and smiles , this story will lead you to love the person in the mirror .

www.ingramcontent.com/pod-product-compliance
Lightning Source LLC
LaVergne TN
LVHW041545060526
838200LV00037B/1143